I Dreamt

of

Tapeworms

in

My Hands

poems for aliens and other lovely creatures

I Dreamt

of

Tapeworms

in

My Hands

Lindsey Nelmar

Published independently.
Original artwork.

TW: Mental illness, self harm.

ISBN: 978-0-578-89844-5

EBook ISBN: 978-0-578-89845-2

Copyright: Lindsey Nelmar 2021

First Edition

This book is dedicated to the shared and overlapping human experience of growing through both lightness and darkness; it is dedicated to whomever feels a connection to it.

This book is dedicated to you and to me.

Introduction

Thank you for being here. Maybe we are friends in real life. If we aren't already, we may as well be soon.

I say that these poems are for aliens and other lovely creatures based solely on how homesick I sometimes feel for no reason - - and that I know I'm not alone in that. I write about taking walks on other planets and seeing the trees from the wind's perspective. I write about sunlight on bare skin, feeling trapped, and sitting comfortably in the grit and dust collected in life's deeper crevices. I write about mental illness, what it feels like to run out of ways to process pain, and reaching maximum capacity. I write a lot about navigation - of places and situations, but mostly people.

....

I never considered myself a poet until a fateful encounter with another Chicago poet. I remember saying, "I am also a writer. Well, I like to write poems sometimes…" He was quick to defend that if you write *anything*, you are a writer in heart, and that is that. "One who writes poetry has a poet's mind." I haven't looked back. I am Lindsey Nelmar; a non-famous-and-totally-fine-with-that poet - a waitress order pad, bus seat poet who has put her first collection together.

I have never read a book of poems from front to back, but I would like to point out that this book is arranged in a particular order. Let these words excite, amuse, startle, or soften you. The lessons and thoughts I have accumulated in my first 26 years will mean whatever they mean or do not mean to you. Here they are - yours for the taking. Please enjoy.

Trigger Warnings: Mental Illness, Self Harm

SPRING

. . . . .

Home

On the South Shore train into Indiana again-
I guess I never leave my apartment soon enough
because beating the train out of the downtown station
is always pins and needles.

Someone two rows ahead
records the streets and houses along
the part of our commute through Chicago's East Side, and
fingerpicked electric guitar soothes me as I ride cross-legged in
denim through the marsh lands of southern Lake Michigan.

The sky is bright and warm again.

How we have missed feeling sun on skin.

Every year's lilac bloom makes me think of Mom and
midnight gardening.

5.5.19

Halfway Bloom

I feel like a halfway bloom
somewhere between closed bud and open flower.

5.29.18

Out of Body

Tonight I saw the trees from the eyes of the wind
and I wept, for in that moment I truly was
free.

11.3.20

Rain Love

Say "goodnight" to the rain
I have listened to all day
like the steady company of a lover who
is here with me but
in the other room
as we, content, do nothing
together.

5.17.20

Playing Detective

People say to listen to your body
as if that entails anything more than hearing
the sound of your breath's exhale
or the gristly friction in a tight joint.

Each gurgling gas bubble
or quickened lub dupp of the heart
can give us insight into how
and what our body is doing.

2.12.20

Untitled

I feel like
I have learned and relearned
and perhaps need to be taught somehow
every day
just how much
our bodies do
for us
with us
without ever having been asked
or ordered.

They just do.

11.10.20

Pandemic Spring

Living in the Twilight Zone -
you couldn't write this shit.
All of the people in this park
are fearful for the same reasons.
I notice we are all watching the
German Shepherd fetching lacrosse balls
like some unspoken group meditation
on something simpler than this.
I eat around the lesioned parts of this apple
that was mealy to begin with
and think about how at home
the sun's warmth feels on my black denim.

4.20.20

Strange Love

I fell a little bit in love with you just now, though I'll likely never see you again,
perfect stranger.
Amongst the patches sewn into your brown corduroy jacket were two from Grand Teton and Yellowstone National Parks, and
straight legged black jeans over well-loved cowboy boots complimented you while I tried to see what book you'd just started.
You sat stoically, separated from ongoings around you in the crowded Saturday morning red line train car.
I can picture you alone on nature walks, listening to birdsong and crunched leaves and quiet wind.
And I wonder where you learned that appreciation, or if you were just born with the salt of the earth between your toes.
I could learn a thing or two from you - I know that much - and maybe you from me if we ever made the time.
We shared a space for less than a minute, and yet I journeyed years with you on wooded back roads and arid desert trails.
We built fires and shared stories of lessons learned and hearts cherished; of making good music and getting tattooed.
You knew how to handle me and helped me be a better version of myself, and I the same for you.
I loved you more than I'd loved anyone, and yet
I wonder who you are.

12.21.19

Garfield Park Conservatory

Plants show us how to practice magic.

They silently and persistently
work in harmony,
carrying water
from sunken roots
through decades-old leaves.

To create a food source from
light waves and basic chemistry
is truly a resourceful
form of art.

Each behaves uniquely,
flowering and not flowering
at its own pace.

Invisible exchanges
trade your exhales for mine
and we all breathe.

4.5.17

Pandemic Square

I untuck my journal from inside the left hand pocket of my denim jacket and set it open across my right thigh which crosses over the other. I am seated on a park bench in an empty and early morning Lincoln Square.
All of the businesses are closed, and it is only birds and no children that I hear here for the first time perhaps ever.
It is too cold to stay long, but I am glad I came.

4.24.20

Unguided Meditation

Putting on a rainfall soundtrack is like screaming at your brain to relax.

1.23.20

Pandemic Philosophy

I brought my copy of "The Daily Stoic" with me to the lake just now, but I'm not even sure what day it is.
What I do know is that the cold spring water feels good on bike ride toes, and the ache in my hips feels strong and alive.

I am having a hard time with stoicism this year.

3.25.20

Juxtaposed to Jupiter

Mars,
I know you
when I see you.
It is as unmistakable as
looking into the eyes
of my own father.

8.19.20

Backcountry Bliss

Drifting breeze
loosens debris
from sturdy needles
of old pine trees
and suddenly
bits of sunlit "stuff"
fall through wooded shadows
like golden rainfall
floating in for landing
softly upon the Earth.

6.20.20

I Never Met You

I never met you, but I often think about you.

When I write something cheeky I am reminded of the weekly column in your local paper that you wrote for those couple of years.
Or in spreading butter and jelly evenly (painstakingly so) to the very edges of my toast only to dunk it into a mug of hot coffee. I've heard for years that this is how you ate toast.

And when I share an adventure or a laugh with my dad, our mutual person, I think about those moments between the two of you.

Like the chaotic evening that resulted in the thwacking of the metal serving spoon that still decades later has a dent in the bottom,
or how he drove you everywhere when your vision started going.

Sometimes I sprinkle you into my day
like rock salt on ice or sugar into tea.
I find places for you to be here with me,
Grandmother.

2.7.19

Introvert at Dusk

Finally,
I rise
to my righteous plateau of mixed emotions,
greeted by these old friends
clothed in cobwebbed robes which sweep the floor
and new ones donning pastel fairy wings
with glimmering strands of silver tinsel
around floaty, dreaming heads.
Those are the ones who pull me giddily toward their day's loot of
joyous moments and winks of stirring eye contact exchanged
with strange passersby
while the cloaked stand firmly in silence as sure as pillars with a
stoic air, like centuries-old redwood trees and their roots who
prove endurance against even the gustiest of pacific winds.
They are all the keepers of each fairy's tether - like kites and
their string holders -
who anchor the swarm of happy honeybees as they drip glitter
onto the ground.
I look around at these creatures and all of the airy vastness
between us here and wonder what happens while I am away;
when buzzing young fairy wings quiet down to tuck themselves
cozily into the pockets of those long woolen robes on ancient
bodies who no longer need the same quantity of sleep,
but who take turns keeping watchful eyes on the tiny dozing
daffodils resting in their softened pockets,
and who tend to this unearthly garden as I am out
and away from this Home.

7.20.19

A Love Note to My Bicycle

On my bike,
I am me,
I am free.

I am strong,
I am agile,
I am fast.

I am confident
and capable
and smooth.

I am fluent
and fluid
and frankly sometimes furious.

I am alone,
I am expressing,
I am moving.

I set the pace,
the direction,
the flow.

I thank my legs
for pushing me home
and the sun
for showing the way.

3.25.20

Shelfful of Journals

Rereading old passages, I find curious patterns
like the two white blankets or how I knew I was going to meet
you exactly nineteen days before I did.

                              God, how much I missed you then.

                                          3.25.20

Observation

Salty sea air cleanses my lungs
and my calves ache from sand running.
The first wave break of Tourmaline Surf Beach is peppered with
a hundred tiny surfers
and I watch them from afar now
collectively drifting south in the water's momentum.

My vantage point lies at the end of Pacific Beach pier where I
look down and ponder how deep it would feel
if I jumped in.
The entire structure beneath my feet
shakes and sways with each booming whitecap,
and the ocean reminds me once again of my insignificance.

1.22.20

Intrigue

Cosmic
bubbles
swirling
morphing
shapeshifting
borderless
colliding
meshing, just briefly
for a moment
in time
we can be
one being
just being
before we split apart again
cellular
meiosis

The hairs on my body
stand at attention
upon the mere mental depiction
of the entire course of you and me
laid out
spelled
phonetically

It makes me scared
to get to know you
at all

4.9.20

Keepsake

I just lit my last pine incense - the one from that gas station in the Red Woods when we were there together.
I am watching the stick disintegrate, its scented coating rising into smoke who carelessly meanders any which way.
Now that the heater stopped blowing, the smoke is no longer faces influence and climbs near perfectly straight upward toward the ceiling.
It burns in the wooden tray on the window sill
and I wonder if it can be seen from the sidewalk
across Western Avenue.

It is cold outside - like it was when we drove back to Chicago.
It will have been one year ago in about two weeks' time.
The temperature changes over the course of that drive were a poetic parallel to what we were going through at the time.
We as passed through each state heading northeast from San Diego, every night on the road was colder than the last.
We were nearing Chicago and nearing our severance from one another.

I have savored this pine incense, not wanting to finish the pack for reasons I cannot pinpoint, though I have some guesses:
- I am afraid to forget the memories of our travels.
- I am reluctant to red my life of all pieces of that time.
- Burning it connects me to the Pacific Northwest

Burning this last stick of pine incense from the Red Wood Forest feels like partial closure from parting ways with you.
I still remember where I kept this pack of incense when we were living on the road - it was in the bottom of three drawers between the driver and passenger seats. Now it sits empty on the

top of all of the trash in my kitchen garbage can in my apartment in Chicago.

The stick is now half gone, its smoke lightly cloaking the room and its contents - myself included - almost as if to comfort me with the lightest touch.

"Goodbye, familiar friend.
Thank you for showing me Chicago."

1.15.18

Farmhouse

The last words
of one of my mothers
rang through me
like the instruments hanging on her wall
when with full attention
and dripping in fire
she called out,
"goodnight, darling."

9.13.20

SUMMER

. . . . .

Benched

This is the first page of an unlined leather-bound journal on the 23rd day of the new decade.

Pacific waves break before me as I watch two small birds pull a piece of something from someone's hocked loogie on the ground. I consider moving.

Sun rays on bare legs feel too good for me to get up again, so I don't.

1.23.20

Cozy

The dog inhales whispered snores
between leg twitches and
the purr of the washing machine comforts me.

"Hommmmme."

1.14.20

Mountain

I woke up today thinking about El Capitan and all of his texture and weight.
How he got there.
The number of ambitious climbers who've either succeeded or failed in summiting his 3,000 feet.
How from the rock's base you can see but a fraction of what an aerial view might offer,
like the quiet geological changes still happening to 100 million-year-old granite.

Zoom out.

Step back.

Notice patterns
and rhythms
and directions
and tendencies.

What might be noticeable only in a bigger picture?

10.7.19

Bicycle Ride

I travel beneath the fiery orange afterglow
of a late August midwest storm.
I am earthbound but barely,
tethered only by a loose curl.

8.24.20

River of Consciousness

> I've filled six pages so far tonight,
> most of them with thoughts of you.

4.23.20

78 Montrose Bus

We were in the back of a 78 Montrose bus that smelled like piss
You sat facing me on the driver's side wearing a dark green
stocking cap that read Brooklyn Brewery in white block letters
and a matching green scarf that looked homemade
You carried a large container with one leftover slice of whatever
pastry that was - what's the occasion?

And I saw you crying
A couple of tears rolled down your face before you buried it
behind the canvass book bag in your lap
I saw myself in you, crying on the bus like that
I always joke that you are not a true Chicagoan until you cry on
public transit at least a couple of times

"Hey, thanks," you said with softened eyes when I told you just
before exiting that I hoped your day got better
And I think we both needed that today

8.19.19

Outside

I like it best when the air is cool but the sun is not;
when surrounding sounds are cricket chirps and the occasional
buzz of a fat, flying honeybee;
when slender trees click together in the wind
like a pile of old bones.

A nearby tree frog's croak reminds me of those
wooden frog-shaped percussion instruments
and how much sonic likeness they really do bear.

I do not need to be inside
when it is like this out here.

7.7.18

Last Night We Built a Fire

Baking the soot smoke out of black denim
hanging on the porch rail
while I alternate sips between
twice nuked coffee and
a modestly hand-rolled spliff.

The men working next door saw
a part of the garage wall?
I don't know, but it's noisy and messy.
Fortunately the wind carries the dust
away from here
and not into my eyes.

There are only about fifteen clouds in the whole sky.

Brisk sunshine begs me to ride a bike
or take a jog
or hop a scotch.

Anything really would feel so nice today.

4.9.20

Writing Prompt: "Misfit"

Misfit
maverick
she was dry-lipped
in a dim lit
bedroom with
some sharp wits
she won't speak to
in a decade
with quarter decks now played
and seeds planted of different spades
but still remembering
the posters on the walls,
that the cat matched the carpet,
and how it felt
to be there.

4.18.20

Early Birds and Recollections

The 4am birds
make me think of you
in the summer of twenty-one when
worries were much fewer and further between
and sunrises kissed us goodnight
more often than not
and I can still recall
the firmness of your mattress
which had lain on the
low-pile carpeting
of your apartment on Milwaukee

4.24.20

Quiet

Tonight after work, I sat on the eighth story roof of a building I don't live in and watched a storm blow over my home town from across the lake.
Very little besides the skyline, the wind, and the occasional bolt of distant lightning was on my mind.
Maybe it was because of the joint I'd just savored.
Maybe it was the quiet molecular pull of the slim crescent moon rising over my right shoulder, squarely between a neighboring church steeple and a cluster of still-bare trees.
Maybe it was neither.

4.7.19

Denim and Atmosphere

Jet black and baby blue,
like raindrops at midnight.
Above the city on my perch,
I start to feel alright.

4.19.20

Hostel

Yoga in the shared space,
breakfast at the ocean,
pelicans floating just above a wave's crest
to "Jai Guru Deva Om."
I reminisce on just this morning.

Francisco and Russ return frustrated from unfulfilled surf.
The Navy HR man from Panama whose name I can't recall
drones on about Atlanta traffic.
A small, grey haired woman brings two paperbacks to the
bookshelf, and I recall the smell of her cooking three days ago.

Yesterday I danced with the ocean
and today I told her "goodbye"
just for now, anyway,
for I'll be here again.

1.26.20

Serenity

Silence
on the tracks -
a sound so seldom, you stop to notice it.
Crickets.
Breeze.
A dog's bark.

Commuters wait for the next train into the Loop,
standing reverently
to the Quiet all around us.

My ears pick up a soft,
steady burble through the trees.

This time it is not
the muffled buzz of Lake Shore Drive traffic.
What I hear instead
is the north branch of the Chicago River say,
"good morning."

8.24.19

Nowhere Man

I realized when I left from
our two full days in bed together
that I was coming back down to earth,
and that's why I liked spending time
with you so much -
because I like where we go
and that we go there together.

3.12.19

You

Were we birds together?

4.19.19

Winnemac Park

I lie
dead weight
in soft grass
on solid ground
and even the exposed parts of my skin
are still comfortable in the breeze
with the help from the sun
who warms me.

4.20.20

My Mother's Bathroom Storage

I just purged and organized all of my mother's bathroom storage.

I stopped halfway through to wonder whether I was doing this as a favor to her or as a means of coping for myself.

                                                                                          I think both.

                                                                                          10.4.19

Showers

I stand naked in a dry shower
with a cucumber face mask resting on suntanned skin.
And I listen
to the lazy afternoon rain landing on back alley pavement
through the dusted screen of the open shower window.
The soundtrack is acoustic guitar at low volume
as I think about my favorite rainstorms.

"Norwegian Wood" comes on and I am now five or seven,
running barefooted through the slick grass in the backyard on a
day my sister and I got along.
It is raining, and we are laughing.
We lie face-up in the grass,
wearing swimming goggles to watch the rainfall.

The piercing chirp of new baby finches
contrasts against the smoothness
of the breeze and rain,
but they are only ever audible at feeding time.

6.11.20

Things I Have Learned Working Hotel Overnights in Downtown Chicago

1. After midnight, many of the nearby east/west running buses converge on the corner of Washington and State between every run. The overnight drivers come into my building for coffee and restrooms. They know my name and I know who takes Splenda. One of them helped an arriving guest with their luggage tonight.

2. People start saying "good morning" around 2:30.

3. Falling asleep on the job is now a real problem for me.

4.4.18

Cherry

So dark outside
that the only light in my eyes
is the glowing cherry just inches from them.

6.27.18

Brother

We are wrapped into the core
of a ball of rubber bands.

9.15.20

Night Ride

I gain acquaintance with
the potholes on Clark just south of Devon
as I imagine the full moon's
naked light
behind neons and LEDs.

8.4.20

I Play Music With My Father

I hear you tune the strings, and
I know we are on for a good session
of transcending into the Sacred Place
of music and freedom and no limits,
where everything goes
and much of it stays.

9.15.20

Out of Towner

White spats
walking back
onstage from the men's room I'd just pissed in
where I didn't mean to offend the waitress
by asking if I should be wary of Jimmy

1.29.20

Pandemic Summer

I leave be the spiders in my shower window
and there's not much happening at all here
with a hollow brain
and the uninterrupted echoes of my helloes
as if I had dropped a brick
in an empty
underground
tunnel

I tune to the droning monotone of the neighbor's A/C unit while
planes descend for landing at O'Hare

One large firework illuminates the sky directly north of here but
leaves me ultimately in the dark
as there are no other lights on

7.10.20

Nostalgic Packrat

These bedroom walls are scattered with pieces of me like I walked in here and exploded
From stolen signs to framed letters, old patches, and photobooth strips from local shows

I sit among them and feel safe.

3.16.20

Memory Jog

Lime popsicles and dusty feet
feel like Mom's house once did,
while the frayed and
chewed-on end of the empty popsicle stick
by an orally fixated anxious tick
feels a bit like Dad's.

6.14.20

Mothering

I think I'd be an okay mother
which I know from having mothered you.

10.2.19

Water Cycle

I am having a humid day
where my brain and my heart are heavy
and dense with the weight of it all.
I am moments away from rainfall,
similarly to the clouds today.

7.19.20

Warm to Cool

The day's sky exhales
a light grey camouflage
in a warm-to-cool gradient,
and the glowing orange space
between the clouds
who block the setting sun
looks like the late afternoon sky
over hot forest fire.

5.23.20

Harvest Moon

With a warm, dim glow cast over us
we reap together
the yield of a summer's bounty.

9.12.20

Dream

Last night I had a dream
that the bottoms of my feet were raw and blistered,
like I'd been running through the desert
barefooted and burning.
I was crawling at one point, unable to stand.

I woke up.

2.25.18

FALL

. . . . .

A Monday

I am feeling again the familiar, dull ache of survivor's guilt
from a good mood
while the two of you are miles away, quietly suffering
the emotional and physical inflictions of a damaged disposition.

. . . . .

I sit on the train eye level to the tightly panted crotch
of a well-groomed man, and I like it.

. . . . .

If I see one more happy couple exchange
"have a good day, goodbye" kisses on this commute,
I am going to start crying right here and now.
These hollow reminders of you have me feeling sick and cynical.

2.24.20

Dying as Someone, Parts I - III

I. I'd crawled to the edge of that sliver of rock peaked out the top of the cliff face to get some breathing room.

And as I sat there cross-legged in the bellowing wind sweeping through the valley floor a thousand feet below me, I imagined falling off of my little perch and the inevitable fatality that would follow. But not in a way like that was what I wanted.

No, this image came with a sense of contentment, like I'd be satisfied with my life thus far if I died in that moment.

I watched my own body travel from top to bottom of this cliff face in perceivably gruesome ways I can skip describing. And I landed at the bottom with a soft, dull thud as the nearby stream trickled on at its same pace, moving in the same direction it already had been.

And I remember feeling so at peace with all of it, resting assuredly that my life was not wasted. That however I was operating as a human being in the world was sufficiently in accordance with my own standards, both by outlook and spirituality.

This was freeing.
This is still freeing.

That particular contentment is a special kind of fuel for me to maintain the kind of personhood I'd be okay leaving behind. For life is not measured to me by length but by depth.

. . . . .

II. This sense of peace reminded me of the time when I was fourteen, drowning, and had run out of air and physical stamina to fight the current anymore. I felt a comforting presence caress me in what I can only describe as soothing love as I neared this life's end that day. I'll never know how my body was freed from that current, as I was no longer conscious to witness the transition. But in dream that night, my late grandfather came to hug me and cry with me. We exchanged no words, only the unspoken understanding that that day was not in fact my death day. It was the only time I'd gotten to meet that grandfather.

. . . . .

III. There is seldom a day wherein mortality stays home from making an appearance in my conscious mind. It reminds me what is worth our sacred, finite life energy. This does not mean that I haven't strayed from reverence for this life, or haven't been too clouded by other things to remember.

It may sound grim to feel okay with dying, but it's really not as scary as people make it out to be.

11.26.17

3.18.21

3.18.21

Forecast

I woke up as heavy as the clouds today,
and both of us cried at the same time.
I rode my bike through a downpour.

6.20.20

Maximum Capacity

It is interesting to me how an emotional callous can thicken and disintegrate at the same time,

as if to reach the point of letting go of something just means you've reached your natural capacity for it.

3.25.20

The Hang of You

You were in a familiar mood this morning - one I've learned very well after 25 years of dancing with you.

4.19.20

Crash

Slipping into the comedown from the last few days' ride along a manic buzz that cleaned the house and baked those cookies and painted that canvass and moved a hundred literal miles.
And I clench the soft things that are wrapped around me as dozens of quiet tears roll down my tired cheeks with snot and sweat and mascara while
I'm short on sleep and soothed only by the same song on repeat.
It hugs me where I need one most,
and it's been on for hours now,
but I refuse to let it go.

It's like a cannonball into a swimming pool
with a running take off
toward the ever almighty leap
to your entire being's crash landing into the unsuspecting flatness
of the still water.
And as you are now submerged,
for a few moments there is no breathing.
Just the muffling encapsulation of the Deep End
as bubbles rise from your earthly frame
past hunched shoulders and up through tangled hair.
And after so many years of cannonballs,
you get more comfortable with the timely process of floating
gently back to the surface
over the struggle to swim upward.

5.7.20

Attempts in Containing the Uncontainable

I hold my spliff under the window
against the screen
as far outside of this room as possible,
kind of like how I hold my love for you
as close to my surface
and as close to my edges
as I possibly can.

8.19.20

Lightyears

I pretend to take walks on Jupiter
who's visible
as I wish that I didn't
think a little bit every day
about dying.

8.14.20

Feeler

I lie on the floor
on my back
on my mat
in this room.

And as I tune into
the pain
felt by so many around me,
and my muscles
begin to lengthen and release,
I shed several
silent tears
for
so

many

people.

11.15.20

Quiet Game

It is in these politicized times
of great tumult
that my brain plays its quiet game
and all of my emotions go to sleep.

Defensive numbness.

1.14.20

Teenager

I'll never forget the summer I fell out of denial that what you had done to me years before was abuse.
Your nine years ahead of my seventeen gave you a head start in achieving what you'd set out to do with me.
Embarrassment that I even found myself in such a position still echoes through the insides of my bones.
My body trembles one time upon a pause to recount some detail, bracing itself for the visceral intensity of each emotion woven through my memory of you.
The muscles that tighten in me are the ones I imagine engage projectile vomiting, but instead of puking, my chest just tightens and I start to cry.
These articles about your recent sexual predator investigation were published almost one year to the day after I finally confronted my memory of you. I am learning in this world that hope for justice is in itself futile, though it still exists tucked around the corners of my mind.
Brushing elbows with pure evil is a fortunately seldom occurrence for me, but you, I believe, were the first reference point on my own barometer. Thank you, Abe, for showing me so young who I need to avoid forever.

4.24.20

(Photo)Synthesize

Like leaves changing,
sometimes it can take a season or two
to understand.

10.27.2019

Draw

I felt so magnetic for a few days,
and now so repellant.

2.9.18

Twenty-Three

You see me here
in my element,
confidently conquering every hurdle that I get.
I smile at challenge, face it head-on, and say, "no problem."
You compliment me on my positive demeanor and my
consciousness of team morale.

What you don't see is at the end of the day
when my oomph is all gone
and I've checked in with all my people
and have completed the day's work
that I'm nearly screaming on the inside,
clinging as I go
to the pieces of positivity
that transpire on the outside
over the course of any day.
Whether it's a joy ride on my bicycle,
a won bet
a kiss under stars
a deep inhale of a flower shop's smell
or a customer's simple satisfaction with my recommendation for
what to order between the chicken farm and the salmon BLT.

. . . . .

It hurts to wake up some days,
and those are the days you see it in my face and you ask me,
"what's up?"
And I wish I had something easily digestible
to say and get off my chest, like
"I had car trouble" or "my mom's dog died."

But no, nothing that is "up" is succinct like that,
so I just don't ever say it.

I can't simply summarize
that for all of my years
on this earth
in this body,
I have lived in a constant state of bearing witness to the
deep emotional torment of the two people who are closest to me
and that I cry sometimes when I think about
the fact that my greatest ever fear is merely
that one or both of them would end their own years
on this earth
in these bodies.
That my favorite form of self destruction
seems to be investing too much into
people I maybe shouldn't
who deplete much of what's left
and leave me more tired,
though too stubborn to leave them
because I've grown too attached
and care about their outcome some how more than my own
a lot of days.

I don't mean for this to be another sob story
which I never do
and that's why I never start it with you
but I carry so much hurt with me where I go,
even on rollercoasters
at concerts
and beach days with friends.
I think about it often and take deep breaths through it when I
do.

So as to keep showing up every day
with that demeanor that you know
and that steadfast, head-on confidence
you think I'm cloaked with
shielded by,
but it's just that - a shield.
One that I take off at the end of the day
as I breathe with my quiet hurt.

7.3.18

Lists for Soothing

Things as certain as ink on paper:

-The simultaneous heaviness and weightlessness of being alone
-How the frequency of my thinking about you has lessened while the intensity of these moments has not
-How glad I am to not have moved further away from home before something like this pandemic happened
-The uncertainty around everything hasn't just begun so much as it has just increased
-My confusingly high level of comfort in crisis and chaos
-Differentiation between the people you see every day and the people who are really there for you

3.22.20
4:31am

Inhale

I inhale the smoke

like I did the smell of you.

4.23.20

Writing Prompt: "Build"

To build anything in a world so full of uncertainty feels foolish and frightening, and somehow necessary.

5.5.20

Logan Square

Patches of my own missing nail polish
remind me of the dilapidated buildings in
"up and coming" neighborhoods
just waiting to be refurbished.
Old haunts in new walls,
check the reviews.
The crowd is different but unoriginal.
I ponder past lives and future stories-
families who've been priced out
and their businesses gone with them.
The new place sticks out
sorely,
like a thumbtack in a pile of fresh cotton.
A rich man's stake in a working class neighborhood;
gentry.

10.4.19

Breathing Room

The beer in my messenger bag was canned not three hours ago, and I can't see the Sears Tower through the dense fog which encapsulates both the skyline and myself. I listen to "Keeping Up" on repeat and befriend the spider on this rooftop where I'm beginning to wonder if the residents of the building next door have noticed the girl in black who comes and sits.
Probably not.

4.23.20

What I Notice Right Now

A handful of the trees around are blossoming white, green, and pink. I bite my cheeks.

The furrow that stays in my brow helps me understand my mother's forehead better, and this frightens me.

4.23.20

Unkown Legend

My work life balance this week is null.
I am tired
and I am lonely
and I ache
everywhere
inside and out.

"This is Damen," says the Brown Line.

"She was an unknown legend in her time," say my headphones.

2.4.19

What Lies Beneath

My face has yearned all day to be peeled back like this

quiet wetness dripping from eyes ever somber

frown roomily outstretched over teeth and cheeks

like a sleepy body spread across fresh bedsheets

. . . . . .

Sometimes this is what rest looks like

6.17.19

Unboundaried Heart

I've been in the position of giving more of my energy (mental, emotional, spiritual, ...) than feels sustainable.

I think my position is both self-assumed and appointed, thus I am trying to reel in my immediate circle.

Here I have this magnificent pie, scratch-made from the finest ingredients, prepared with care and baked with exquisite love. I give some to everyone in my life. I give a small amount to friends and larger portions to my family.

I give extra - 2, sometimes 3 portions each - to some who seem to need it more. I am convinced one or two of them could starve to death without it.

I myself do not get a whole piece, but I am able to lick the crumbs from the empty pan and can still taste and savor my beautiful dish. These crumbs taste like ginger face masks and quiet time when no one is around. Sometimes I wonder what a whole piece would look like - maybe I'd have more art to be proud of or a more advanced yoga practice. My physical and emotional health would certainly be stronger. For now until I learn how to better balance this, I share too much with everyone who needs it because I do not know the middle ground between here and standing idly by.

11.9.18

"I need your energy,"

...you'd included in your invitation.

I feel like everyone in my world is leaning on me right now - like I have one hand against the earth and the other holding up so many people.

I am so empty.

I can't tell if what I feel is sad or tired or losing or depleted.

All of it.

Much of my energy is far removed from me these days.
Today I will reel that energy back inward and focus on tending to my replenishment.

I am welcoming the ebb and flow.

9.12.19

Mother

Is this what you felt like?
Did you, too, feel like a tired lioness
as I listened to you crying behind closed doors?

I know you more
and blame you less
with each passing day.

8.21.20

Hardening

I am understanding
the slow becoming
of Furiosa
now more than ever.

She is so independent
perhaps out of resentment
of all of her dependents
leading up into the fury.

She is an empath
at her core,
connecting deeply,
navigating well,
usually.

There is a callous on her soul
which no longer
lets the light out,
and she carries differently now
the burdens of her people.

6.3.20

Kaleidoscope

What do you do when you love only some pieces of a person?

Do we learn to love them, tolerate them,
or protect ourselves from them?

Who gets to stay?

11.13.20

Uncool Patterns

You can keep kicking me in the ribs and
saying "sorry" afterward, or
you could just stop kicking me in the fucking ribs.

7.29.20

Learning Experience #25286

Last night I went too far again;
crashed my bike and slept outside.

I woke up soggy with sweat and shame.

7.29.20

Ace Bandage

Candy-coated demons
who stink of bad decisions
echo hollow swelling
across a folded frame

9.30.20

Levels

It's days like these I wonder if I do need the meds.

If my crooked brain really does need chemical help again,
or if I can manage my mental health without it.

I think about all of the things I spend my time on
and which ones help
and which ones don't.

I could use adjusting.

7.30.18

Distant

I feel a familiar kind of loneliness today -

the one which feels particularly close to good friends

but extra far from everyone else in the world.

It is a sweet and sad feeling

wherein I am lightyears away from

here.

10.26.18

Steady Growth

I find myself ready for the steady growth to slow
with its ebbing pains
I look around at you and notice that
maybe it never does

Is there a plateau?
I hope it won't always feel so avalanche.

I am hit against a wall
like a pacific coast wave
crashing sideways into a '68 Turner longboard
Breath knocked out
and we coast, but just briefly

Learning the goodness of the scrapes and bruises,
I hold near the fear and heartache

A point on the horizon draws closer
I feel a new leaf turning
In this moment I feel allowed to rest
and I wait for the other shoe to drop

6.15.19

Little

You're a little kid
still so jaded your soul could be two hundred and five.
I don't believe I'll ever know whether the patience I have for you is too much or too little.

Little is what I often feel
not just due to mere birth order but also to shrunken accomplishments. It took two months to tell you that I was back in school, completely by accident even, mostly out of fear for making even the littlest of waves.

I feel a little like a broken record
when I think about your very big episode on the drive to Great America. It was maybe 2003 and while I've always sympathized with the fullness of your plate at any given time, what I experienced in the car with you that day made me feel very little.

Very little is said between us some days.
Frequently occurring gaps in conversation drive us both to go rummaging through our brains for any shareable food for thought. I live here and you live there. You watch that and I watch this. Food, hobbies, beliefs, passions..
The overlap is little.

I've always had a very big interest
in feeling important or capable. Getting a laugh, setting the test curve, or any kind of public recognition has always satisfied a part of me - the questionably little part of me that very much likes feeling big.

11.25.19

Untitled

I'm lying in sweatpants on my bed
overeating pistachios.
I'm drunk and I just spent nearly three hours
on my nails. I do them meticulously, as you once pointed out.

I heard from you today.
You'd been on my mind for the last couple of weeks
and sometimes always.
I'd wanted to reach out to you.
You beat me.

Something inside me wants to not get this job.
Probably because I know that moving on would be so much
easier without further rooting.
Because I know that committing to anything new will slow down
the process of leaving.
I like to be able to leave.

My upper back is aching.
It's a dull rhythmic discomfort between my shoulder blades only
lower, slightly. It was probably the three hours I spent doing my
nails.

I'm lonely in a cosmic sense
like none of my people are near me
and this makes me miss the west coast.
Hearing from you makes me yearn for it harder.

I think about my path from here to where I want to be
and I panic at its lack of clarity.
The first time I got anywhere near there, I was dusty and van
dwelling. It's hard to tell where any of this could fit into
something like that.

9.4.19

Bicycle / Work Day

My hips pay for the sins of their keepers,
straddling the line between riding and being ridden.

- - / / — — —- ~

My tired back aches
from heavy lifting of the day
and I sing the same praise
of "Little Green" and purple haze.

3.12.19

Whiplash

I thought for some reason
that I was getting played all along.
And come to find out,
I was kind of right
but with so many shades of grey
that I can't even tell.

And now I sit in this wake
alone
exactly how I started
only sadder.

The callous thickens
along with the plot.

I knew better.

12.5.18

The Narcissist and the Empath

Parts of me
admittedly
derive sick pleasure
from knowing how alone you are.
Particularly
those parts of me
which have clouded under calloused skin
and the glue and mud
which I had to call upon
in mending myself
back to working order
after you
took a bludgeon to my psyche.

                                                     Parts of me
                                                     however
are still sad for you-
as sad as they have
always been
for you.
They are the parts of me
who are blindsided by intensity as palpable as yours
They are the same parts of me
which hope for you
and Others Like You
to grow out of the states of being
which make you so dangerous
to Others Like Me
who must learn the hard way
about these traps set
for soft souls.

8.6.20

Colonizer

In body, mind, and heart,
I've been inhabited by you.
Have you done this out of malice,
or narcissism,
or frank and honest curiosity?
Could you sense some kind of susceptibility in me
for your greedy talons to grab hold?
Did you think about my place in all of this before you decided to enter
and influence
and conquer
and damage?
Or were you merely pondering your own amusement when you knew you couldn't stay
and that I couldn't either?
Come to find out- this dyad is in fact a triad,
very much unwilling,
and I am somewhere on the outskirts in between
the two of your manipulative, twisted minds.

She asks me how I'm doing.
"What's going on in your life?"
And I want to say, "your boyfriend."
Instead we agree that we are both presently annoyed with someone in our lives, and I'm almost positive they're both you.

How much does she know?
Who's testing me more here?
Get out of me - both of you.

Get out of me.

12.13.18

Poison

The other day I realized that what you're doing, what I'm experiencing here with you, is emotional abuse.
You love having this power - I think back on the strategic questions you've asked me in strange contexts and how they'd been designed to paint me as vulnerable to you from the start. Realizing that and how fucking angry it makes me is enough drive for me to take that power away from you.
My heart is not your muse.
She can have you.
I don't want you.
You are poison, and I will no longer interact with you as if you aren't.

And you're a shitty boss.

12.18.18

F Street

Dried crumb
discarded
brushed unflinchingly
onto the floor
like a spare grain
of semolina in your kitchen
which does not burn like flour does,
I'll always remember you telling me.

4.22.20

Drip

Spilt out of a covered head,

my skin has tears to catch.

11.13.20

Due Back Soon

I am
a library book
checked out
for a time
skimmed
consumed
returned
upon having served
some kind of purpose

Ghosts of
dog eared pages
and notes on margins
in strange handwriting
are all that seem to occupy me
some days
as I collect the dust
of every place
I've ever searched
for home

8.30.20

Afterglow

I am warmed
from my guts to my skin
in what could be pleasure
or what could be pain
over you-
both of them
and every hue in between

I lie back
on my bed
feet still touching the floor
only to have one thing which grounds me
to this plane
for the surreality is blinding here
in these dim fairy lights
as one of you called them
and the salt lamp
that glows me to sleep nowadays
while I wonder if yours is still missing
the top two of its three lightbulbs

Get that fixed-
it (quietly) drives me nuts
and suddenly I miss it

3.18.20

Easy Tiger

If stripes earned look like
mascara lines down chilled winter cheeks
or failed lovers in clean bedsheets
then I've certainly become more decorated
in the time that I've known you.

2.1.20

Carelessly Dangerous Leaders

I lie awake
too early again
and choking on stale fumes
of palpable resentment
that I wish would leave my tongue
with brushed teeth but
has stained the flavor of my mouth
anymore.

8.28.20

Pandemonium

I am restless
I am half dressed
in this time of distrust
and disgust
with one another
from our unkempt
corners of this shared space
before we enter the void
or not
no one knows
really

4.22.20

Quarantined

This is shit.
I have nothing new -
just a different progression
of the same goddamned songs
in the same space
curated nicely, I must say.
It feels nice in here
for losing your mind.

4.22.20

Face Shield

Breath like bullets-

                                              breathe to kill.

11.14.20

Dream: Glass Factory

Pull me upright
before this towering sand mine.

He's got us cornered
in this haunted loft
laced with dust and artifacts,

and he watches
from behind the glass
to see how much we buy of it.

11.14.20

Her Eyes

…are both brown and blue,
believed by indigenous cultures
you've said
to have vision into
both spirit and physical realms.

I wonder what is in my eyes
so brown
to see all that they see.

2.6.18

Early Quarantine

I lie in silent near-pitch-blackness after watching the sunset via the slow gradient of light washing my bedroom walls

I count the stripes of pale blue light from a nearby flood lamp sneaking in between my slatted blinds.
Why do they seem to underline the simultaneous autonomy and hollowness of being alone?
There are 47 of them.

I wonder how long and how severe this will be.
How used to this we could have to grow to be,
at least for a little while.

This surreality feels harsh and bleak,
like the barren, bright white salt flats of New Mexico.
I never saw them in person - not yet, anyway.

Positivity is here.
I can feel it.
And generally I can see it.
But today I am having a harder time at doing so.

I lie with silent near-pitch-blackness in its stead,
at least for a little while.

3.23.20

WINTER

. . . . .

Afraid

I'm feeling depressed again,
but this time I'm less afraid.

9.26.16

Glue Trap

Dead spider on a glue trap
I lie unmoving and unable to uncurl
the heavy twist of limp limbs
which is fixed to the soft knit
of a wool blanket
under goosebumped skin

Entangled in my own web
of long arms around a tired head
and hair still wet and uncombed
a piece of which
on the gasping inhale of a loud sob
catches in my throat

Reptile filled with cold blood
basking in the warmth of a heat lamp
just reversed, for I am
a warm creature
soaking in the cool and quiet sadness
who looms above and around me
this time as far as I can see
There is no dappled light
coming through this moment's cloud
only the familiar dense suffocation of a
hard day

6.28.20

Breaking-In a Broken Heart

I lie alone
under the crushing new weight of this quarantine
and how lonely I was even before it.
The thought of lifting my head,
let alone getting up from this bed,
is exhausting.
I lie curled
into my left side
with my face resting against the inside of my folded arm and I
think about how good it feels
to pretend
it's someone else's body I am resting it on.

3.25.20

Whirlwind

Myself and I are on a haunted island,
accompanied only by the chatter of neglected teeth
and the curls who hug this dizzy head.

9.16.20

To Bear Witness

Mental illness is like the heaviest blanket imaginable.

You have to carry it around on top of you,
using up your hands and their ability to hold;
consuming your focus and ability to think;
making it difficult to walk
or interact with the world outside of the blanket.

Watching someone you love move through life under their heaviest blanket is like
having a wound that does not heal.
It bleeds for them.
It reopens every day whether you're near them or not.
The wound cannot scab over and heal if the illness has not been addressed, treated, or reigned in.
The wound brings heartache as you look at it and remember how their suffering is tenfold of yours while you merely watch.

Sometimes being a lifeline to someone and their heaviest blanket requires building an emotional wall of your own
for protection and self preservation.
But you remember that that is a privilege-
that people cannot build an emotional wall from themselves or their own heaviest blanket.
Though many try, I suppose.

. . . . . .

I just don't know how to help or what to do sometimes-
when the good and the joy cannot be seen from beneath the bulk of weighted knit.

6.28.18

Early 20's

It's hard to be a lighthouse in the eye of a hurricane.

· · · · ·

        Cross state lines in the middle of the night

            · · · · ·

                You don't have to work at a hospital
                        to live on-call at the E.R.

                                  Various

Estranged

You couldn't possibly know
what this does to me
every time
after these half dozen cries of "wolf"

I get a call
I learn of crisis
and then nothing -
radio silence

And I am preparing
both mentally and physically
for the worst

The first time was nauseating
I sat on the floor in my boss's empty office
and cried until the room stopped spinning
long enough to make the next move
from where I sat at my hotel front desk job

The second time
was when I worked at the restaurant in Old Town -
the only time I ever saw them transfer a table to another server
I was on an outbound train in a matter of hours

The only two emotions I remember
from my bike ride on Wednesday are
bravery and fear

I felt brave to be here again
and broaching the front lines
only after having done a ritual or two
(I've learned by now to prepare my Self)

Fear was what followed shortly upon realizing
I had no idea what to expect of this
erratic behavior and lashing out
Should I not have come here alone?

I am realizing now that not once have I ever been asked
to drop everything and save anyone -
not one time

I have assumed this role,
have woven it into the stitching of my parts
from the deeper crannies of my heart
and its love for you

But in bearing witness to my own part in this
I have no choice but to draw my bridge to you
To what degree, I'm not sure I'll know for a while
I have exhausted
every avenue of support

I have exhausted
my capacity for absorbing these blows of yours

And so while you say that this book I'm working on
is a mere compilation of the conversations I am
"too afraid to have,"
perhaps there is some truth to that

It is a fear adjacent to the one I felt
when you called me on Wednesday
angry for having knocked

This book is me taking up the space
I was always afraid to occupy
in its bearing too much weight
on these eggshells here

4.9.20

Strong, Not Weak

Today I was proud to make it to the grocery store and back.

We say "I love you" now more than ever since that weekend in the hospital room. He'd told me on the way there that I had to be strong because he wasn't capable of being strong enough for all three of us.

I aged twenty years that weekend.

"I am not upset with you or here to judge you. I just need to know what happened," I'll always remember explaining. It was the first time I ever had no choice but to be assertive. It was up to me whether or not she would be admitted to the hospital, as if that was good judgement on the psych evaluators part.

"What is your opinion?" He asked me - the twenty-four year old in shock and under pressure.

"Excuse me?"

11.8.18

"In a Bad Way"

…has come to mean much more to me than just
"not doing well."

It means "in a mode that is bad, actively"
and there is something to be done
about and around it.

For someone is not just
in a way that is bad
and also able
to navigate their surroundings -
no.

The deep torment of this "way"
is a testament
to how much support they could really use.

9.26.20

I'm Relieved to No Longer Feel This Way

I've been thinking that success is not really in my cards in this life. I don't think I'll ever live up to my dreams. Merely surviving in this goddamn role requires so much energy that there isn't much leftover to truly thrive.

I'm okay with this because I know so many people are in a similar circumstantial boat. But I'm also annoyed by this, as I feel capable of so many good things in this life.

I feel robbed.

1.6.19

Sometimes

…But no one asks how I am.
I don't tell anyone because no one asks.

And the truth is: I'm not always fine.
I'm getting by, and I'm successful enough in doing so that people don't seem to worry.
But everything on my plate - everything I think about in a given day - keeps me bent. I stay bending in hopes that I don't break, though sometimes I can imagine it.

1.5.19

Release Valve

Today I thought about cutting my skin
just to drain some of the pain beneath it.

I didn't, but I would.

4.22.20

May Day

Still in bed for the fourteenth hour

The day is bright and perfect for adventure
I contemplate taking my camera on a bike ride but lose interest.

I am so tired.

I receive a text containing
time and date details of the upcoming surgery.

I look at prices of used van conversions that I can't afford.

I roll back over,
burying myself for now in just blankets.

5.6.19

Yoga Practice

…and as I started crying in my resting pose,
I rolled onto my right side
for some semblance of privacy,
even though everyone is home,
and I am lying in the living room floor.

I stayed there, still,
with my flowing tears over this deep loneliness,
thinking about how poetic it was
to be crying in a shared space
after longing so strongly
to feel witnessed.

4.22.20

Growing Pains

Cherry flavored poison
puckers in my mouth
and warms my flesh
as the moss in my lungs
hangs weight from my eyelids.

Folded pocketknife in my shower,
don't ask why.
"Love yourself
when your ankles itch
from the last time you didn't,"
I write down for myself.

This unflattery gets me nowhere,
and I hate myself for it.
What comes most naturally, right now, to me
makes me want to not be me.

6.11.20

Cover Me Up

There's skin in the teeth of my pocketknife again
and soreness where I drained some pain
strategically from a place where clothing lies protectively.

I don't know how I'll explain it to you.

I have run out of spaces to tuck away my hurt.

9.16.20

Nap

Lifeless
are my sails who hang without wind
as I lie here
in a pile of soft and grey

11.16.20

Family Tree

Only on the tree of my own
would I keep extending hands
only to get bitten.
And so here we are
perched on the same branch
while one of us is bleeding
and both of us ache.

9.23.20

Feeble Friday

Ill-timed firework
pull the trigger in a dark room
now I'm found in slices
and spread across vices

Quiet cries of cherry jam
leak from paper skin

9.16.20

Twenty-Four

It was almost like a partial resuscitation.

She's a moth circling too closely to a light too bright to ever fly away from.
I just gave her a piece of me to last another day,
like a part of my guts were sucked out of my trunk by a vacuum hose down my throat.

I feel lighter.
I mourned it.
Or maybe I mourn for the circumstances, but I cry.
A dam broke when that piece was removed - no, given - and received.

It is my place, I feel, to give life to my life-giver
when she needs it.

10.30.18

Mom and Dad

I took a nap in your car in her driveway.

My skin burns at the sites of new stripes.

The day is sunny,
my disposition is not.

I drag to Chicago in the backseat
my guilt for not being better company.

9.16.20

Fuzzy

I stay looming
in my own elected fog,
everlasting like the sadness it is only softening.

5.7.20

Birthday Girl

I rode cloud nine all the way home
from my birthday where I'd been convinced that
I wasn't as alone on my island as I always seem to feel

A text message from far away,
surprise cookies,
a friend visit,
and decorations filled my heart.

And for several blissful moments I was joyful
until behind the bedroom door that had just surprised me with
Halloween themed birthday decorations,
greeting me, too,
were the remains of my most recent episode
of bloodied skin and whiskey straight.

It feels dirty.

10.25.20

Even Though I was Drunk

The flashbacks are no less vivid
of the whiskey-scented brand of
misdirected blind rage who
tripped me into self-loathing;
this time to the point of
full-speed slashing and
panicked blood-stopping.

I needed stitches.

Instead I called my mom from my bathroom floor.
I tried to sound normal but probably didn't.

The nurse at urgent care the next morning sent me to the E.R. for those stitches and a psych evaluation.

Instead I went to Walgreens for butterfly bandages and gauze, and then home to cry and sleep for the next four or five days. My temporal and monetary budgets only allowed for urgent care this time.

Only centimeters of translucent tissue remained between the blade of my Smith and Wesson and the big, bluish vein in my forearm's underside.

I nursed those four wounds with such diligence and care, like the world's most delicate wild orchid. I talked to it while its layers grew in over the following weeks and fused the loose ends of skin back together. I sang it songs and told it how simultaneously sorry I was and how proud of their growth I felt.

Happy birthday.

3.31.21

The Ebb and Flow

This is some form of rock bottom
wherein the swelling has gone down in my tired eyes,
but plasma still weeps from the gashes in my flesh.

10.26.20

Truth Hurts

For a few days I felt badly for not protecting you from the truth
of my accident

until I remembered that you never protected me from much of
anything.

11.16.20

Untitled

The fibers in my punching muscles tighten
as I am pummeled by this Mavericks wave
of intense self hate.
I am inspired to imagine
plunging with a steady fist
the blade of a serrated steak knife
deep into the far side of the pits of my guts
and sawing myself in half.
I hear the sounds.
I feel the meat.

But I am tired of letting the weight on my heartstrings
manifest into bruises that ache when I chew.
I am tired of counting the days it takes
for pools of purple blood to disperse from my skin
back into my heart.

I have shed so many tears for the hollow memories of self
inflicted pain that this beautiful body has been dealt to carry for
the rest of its life with me.

I have no choice but to nurture
a complicated friendship
with the perceivably shame-colored markings on my arm,
who are here with me forever now.

I have returned to this lessons enough times,
that the grief alone is enough to soften my own blows.
Nothing feels as bad as abuse,
and nothing in this world deems worthy
the abuse of the self by the self.

The scabs who formed those one hundred days ago just to cover
and protect me, and make me whole again;
they didn't do it in vain.

1.23.20

(Hard and) Soft

Ten days before my accident,
we'd dressed up and gone on a date to the newly reopened Leather Museum, followed by a walk through our favorite cemetery.

In all of our pandemic romance, this was the most dressed up you'd seen me. I felt powerful in that outfit with its nicely silhouetted collection of black textures - denim, knit, and fur. Those black and white (faux) snake skin stilettos have not been worn nearly enough - yet.

I was looking for a photo of the collage I made last fall when I rediscovered the photos from that day. We were joyous and light, all things considered. Your dad had died five months prior and for a multitude of reasons, it was work finding moments of happiness. You looked smitten with me, and I looked carefree. We both smiled cheeky smiles in the photos, of which we took many because I brought my Nikon that day.

Seeing photos from then or earlier brings such bittersweet feelings to my eyes, as I long for the innocence of us to come rushing back somehow, like the memories do of every unflattering state of mine you've bewilderedly borne witness to since. I'm so sorry you've had to see me be violent with me. I'm so sorry I've had to see me be violent with me.

Not that I haven't grown, both separately and in conjunction with you. I have done more fleshing out and tending to emotional sore spots here with you than I have ever done - I think thanks in part to how inherently vulnerable this makes me feel. I love you a jarring-to-me amount, but I'm becoming much more used to that.

I can never undo the heartache I added to your year.

But in the growing grand total of our time spent together, I like to think that the love and comfort we co-create is both full and soft enough to cradle and cushion the sharp spikes of these hard times - like a jar of nails resting amidst a pillow made of dew drops or a ring of barbed wire tucked into a mess of multi-colored feather boas.

3.10.21

Anatomical Appreciation

I haven't shown my hands enough gratitude,
for it is only of their own dexterity by which I wash my dishes
and push myself from the ground
and whose help I call upon to tighten the screws of my glasses.

. . . . .

I have witnessed over the last few weeks the slow and steady
regrowth of flesh between two edged of torn skin.
It started with a sort of polka-dotted mesh which multiplied in
layers, cell by teeny tiny skin cell.
It was a project my body took on involuntarily but out of the
grace and kindness of its mere genetic makeup.
The magic of regeneration is lost in a scab.

11.22.20

Untitled

Guilt is the heart wishing it could do something.

4.19.21

Could Have, Should Have

Sometimes I mourn who I would have been without you.

9.25.20

Preparation

Forgive my wall who builds itself
for I just want to feel safe.

4.21.21

I Dreamt of Tapeworms in my Hands

...an older woman pulled and pulled
and pulled them
from pin-pricked holes in the centers of my palms;
and I could feel them unraveling from beneath my skin,
and she freed them from the hollows of my hands,
and freed my hands from the tangles of the worms.

                                                Liberation of an unpleasant kind.

I woke up with my palms stinging.

                            7.14.19

SPRING

. . . . .

Unpacking

Of the stories that we tell ourselves - - which ones are true?

. . . . .

Whose words litter my mind and mouth?

. . . . .

Do they feel like home to my ears?

. . . . .

These sound like you, not me. No more airtime.

11.13.20

A Lesson From Massage School

A "trigger point" is a hyper-irritable spot within a taut band of muscle - a specific group of fibers essentially frozen in a firing state of tense restriction.
A trigger point might not even be felt by its carrier until it is provoked or agitated, thus causing pain or even limiting mobility. When trigger points are massaged out of the body; discomfort eases, muscle function is restored, and sometimes local trauma is healed in that area.
Working through trigger points is painful.
It can bruise you or bring you to tears.
But finding the trigger points and doing the hard work to get through them is what sets your body free of pain and suffering.

The same of what is true in the physical body is as true in the spiritual body.
Within our navigation through the world around us, sore spots of tense emotion inevitably build up and lie below the surface, waiting and ready to be brushed up against accidentally or bravely explored.
Like skilled and savvy hands undo dissonance in our soft tissue, proper tools and preparation can be helpful in digesting emotional and spiritual tenderness.
Just as pain receptors work to notify us for trouble in the physical body, emotions exist in part to help us identify and locate these sore spots within our minds.

11.25.19

Outgrow

People talk about evolution in its past tense, like it isn't something still happening all around us.
As if humans stopped evolving once they started walking upright.

But socially, culturally, personally we are evolving every day, year, and generation.

We learn what to do and not do differently.

We learn what is dangerous, foolish, fulfilling, or wise.

If we're lucky, we get to keep what works and leave what doesn't.

There is a lesson in every situation, in every moment, in every success, and in every error - every lost opportunity or those never granted in the first place.

. . . . .

I started writing the first half of this piece in 2018 and am finishing it now as I conclude the arc of this book,
having done a difficult and healing amount of reflecting as I put each chapter of my truth together like this.

Some of our best evolution comes out of sitting down and being honest with where we've been and how it feels to have been there.

The seed might not enjoy the pressures and darkness of being buried underground. But from those pressures form the seedling who then sprouts, perhaps nervously at first, into the bright sunlight cast on this bountiful earth who has all that the growing plant could ever need.

11.16.18 - 3.18.21

New Day

I rise
at sunrise
and breathe the deep belly breaths
of a new day;
both feet planted
in fresh January soil,
curious to grow always
but feeling readier
this day.

1.29.20

The Moon Cried Wolves into the Night

She rested
only with the peace of mind
that the Earth was there to hold her.

11.1.20

I Used to Write About

...feeling only half-lit or not yet fully bloomed.

> "There is only so much power in one half-lit being whose own road to being whole has detoured through more circles of hell than she'd care to admit - mostly to herself..."
>
> -August, 2018

I am still not fully illuminated nor have I completely blossomed (don't get me wrong - I am not complaining when I observe this idea. For one to ever feel such a way in any given lifetime is certainly a blessing, but arguably a fallacy. Can't we all keep unfolding forever?).

But I used to think that it was up to other people to make me feel more brightly lit or fully bloomed. It wasn't until I journeyed deeper into the darkest center of the underground seed of my soul that I learned it wasn't anyone else's place to do - it was a matter of my own doing.

I have felt my shadow brush up against me; I have heard myself approaching and I have run the other way. I have leaned with naivety into the quicksand of denial and pretended all was well when I could feel that it just wasn't.

I never listened to the ugliest, most unapproachable sides of me until they gave me no choice but to.

There will always be more to learn and uncover - sometimes it might be frightening and sometimes it might be lonely.

But it's not up to them - it's up to you.

3.10.21

Homecoming

I dreamt that a spider freed me from my own web,

and a sled dog pulled me home.

12.29.20

Author's Note

I'd toyed with the idea of publishing a small collection of writing for about two years before I lost my job in 2020 and found myself actually having time for it. In truth, I knew I would need something to keep my head above water during the dreadfully un-engaging, unemployed Covid-19 winter. And so I set out to self-publish a book of all of the "keeper" poems up until my 26th birthday - an arbitrary but decisive benchmark of time to work with. But the year at hand (for so many reasons- some not mentioned, if you can believe) compounded with years prior, had culminated into the events discussed in the darkness of the winter chapter, and it all felt too relevant to exclude from this project. Suddenly I had more work cut out for me with this book, as what had started as a directionless retrospect of older material wrote itself in real-time to be more of a story about overcoming, and learning new depths of my own human spirit.

Gathering this body of work at all, but especially at the time that I started it, was in itself amusing, occasionally daunting, and deeply cathartic. It went quickly from "just for fun" to intensely helpful. And I'd like to make abundantly clear that with a stellar support network, leaning into healthier habits and coping mechanisms, and a rockin' therapist; I am fortunate to have the resources I need.

One of my greatest intentions with sharing my truth like this is to reach out and touch anyone who may have ever felt similarly, or even lonely in these experiences. You are not alone. There are more resources out there for mental health every day. We are stronger than we think we are, and more special than we can often see. There is Love in this world for you.

www.ingramcontent.com/pod-product-compliance
Lightning Source LLC
Chambersburg PA
CBHW031250290426
44109CB00012B/512